Mastering Art
DRAWING

Anthony Hodge

STARGAZER BOOKS

CONTENTS

© Aladdin Books Ltd 2005

New edition published in the
United States in 2005 by:
Stargazer Books
c/o The Creative Company
123 South Broad Street
P.O. Box 227
Mankato, Minnesota 56002

Designer: Phil Kay
Editors: Jen Green,
         Harriet Brown
Drawings: Anthony Hodge
Illustrations:
Ron Hayward Associates

Printed in UAE
All rights reserved

Library of Congress Cataloging-in-Publication Data

Hodge, Anthony.
    Drawing / Anthony Hodge.-- New ed.
        p. cm. -- (Mastering art)
    Includes index.
    ISBN 1-932799-01-X (alk. paper)
        1. Drawing--Technique--Juvenile literature. I. Title.

NC730.H536 2004
741.2--dc22   2004040156

Introduction

Drawing has a wonderful quality of immediacy, of something that is happening now. Its great advantage is that it can be done almost anywhere. With a sketch pad and pencil you need never be bored.

Starting with basics

This book aims to develop your natural talents and ideas. We examine the range of materials available. We look at some of the basic skills of drawing. Then these skills are used in a series of projects. We will explore sketching techniques and work toward more finished drawings. We will examine how simple forms can be developed into more complex ones. The main emphasis is on drawing what you see, but there are projects that involve working from photographs and from your imagination.

Making connections

There are no hard and fast rules about how to draw, so try not to be too critical of your work. Drawing is about looking carefully and developing an understanding of what you see.

▶ "On the opposite page you can see some sketches I made at the zoo, using a black felt-tip marker. Whatever you feel about animals being kept in captivity, zoos are a wonderful place to draw."

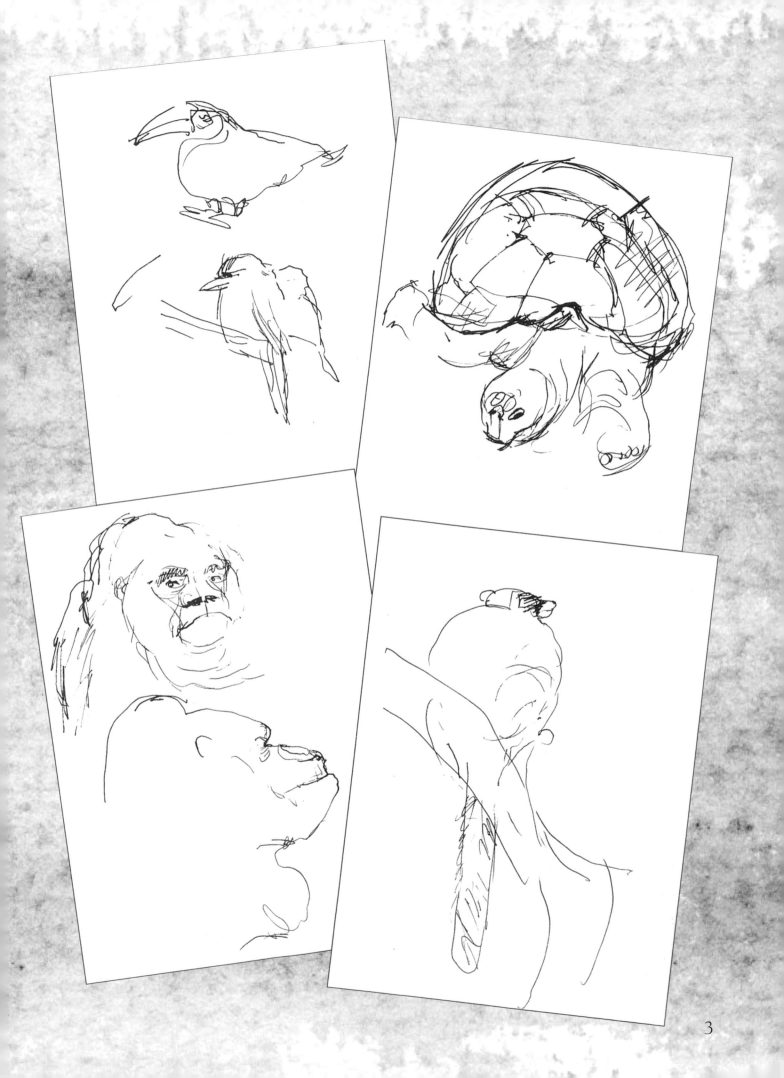

3

Pencil, Pen, and Wash

Drawing involves making marks, and there are plenty of different tools you can use to do this. All drawing materials are made of particles of color, or pigment, bound together with a different kind of gum, or medium, to perform different jobs. These first pages are about getting to know the tools and trying out as many as possible.

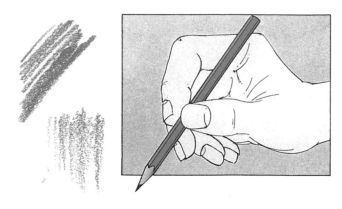

What feels most comfortable?

You will find some tools suit you better than others. Most people feel safer with a pencil than with a brush full of ink, because they feel they have less control with ink. Later, you may come to enjoy the hit and miss element of drawing with a brush.

Getting equipped

Collect as many different kinds of tools as you can. It is not always necessary to buy expensive, new equipment. Look for any unwanted bits and pieces that friends or relatives may have. The projects that appear later in this book are made in materials that are appropriate to the subject or style of the work.

Pencils

Pencils are the basic drawing tool. Within the wooden tube of a pencil is the pigment, graphite, mixed with the medium, clay. Pencils are graded according to the hardness of the graphite. A graphite pencil marked HB is a good all-purpose tool. For a thicker, softer line, you can use anything from a 2B to a 6B.

 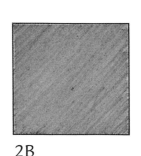 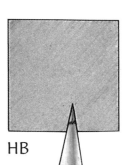  

4B   2B   HB   2H   4H

Pen and ink

India ink is a good, strong, black medium and can be used with a drawing pen, or fountain pen, or with a brush. Felt-tip markers are also widely available. Their range of expression is limited because they make an unvarying mark. Rotring pens are used for technical drawings.

Pen and wash

To make a wash you need a brush that holds plenty of ink and water. First, make a drawing with pen and ink, and let it dry. There are two kinds of ink, permanent ink and non-waterproof ink. If your drawing is in permanent ink, the hard pen lines will contrast with the soft shadows of the wash.

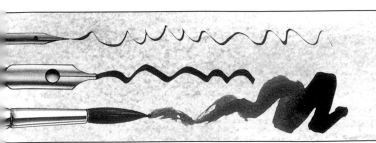

Nibs

Nibs for ink pens vary in size and thickness and, of course, the lines they make vary accordingly. Marks can also be made in ink with a paint brush.

Charcoal, Conté, and Crayon

Getting a grip

How you hold your drawing implement makes a big difference to the kind of line you produce. If you hold your implement in the middle in a relaxed way, your arm muscles will relax, and the line you produce will be relaxed, too. If you hold your implement near the point, you can produce harder, more intense marks. Try holding it at the end, to produce freer, looser marks.

Sharpening your pencils

Pencils can be sharpened with a pencil sharpener or with a sharp knife. You can also use sandpaper to vary the point: a sharp point for fine lines, and a flat edge for thick lines.

Getting some support

Even if your paper is in a pad, it may not be stiff enough to give you proper support. You will need to rest your paper on a board. You can get one from an art store, or buy a piece of plywood, or fiberboard from a hardware store.

Charcoal

Charcoal is made from burnt wood, usually willow, and is always black. It is available in sticks of various thicknesses, which are brittle and tend to break. Charcoal is also available in *compressed* form, in a straight, hard stick, or in pencil form.

Fixative

To protect your drawings from smudging—especially charcoal and pastel drawings—spray them lightly with fixative.

Erasers

There are many different kinds of erasers. For chalk or charcoal drawing, use a kneaded eraser, a soft gray eraser that you can squeeze like clay.

Conté

Conté is a hard form of pastel compressed into a thin stick. It traditionally comes in black, white, and shades of brown, although other colors are available. Drawing with brown rather than black conté can produce a softer, warmer drawing.

Wax crayon

Crayons are bold sticks of color. They can sometimes be dissolved with turpentine or mineral spirits, and applied with a brush or cotton. Used on a textured surface, crayons produce a grainy effect that can add considerable interest to drawings.

What kind of paper?

Cartridge paper is fine for most pencil or ink drawings. Try out other kinds too, including colored paper. Textured paper is good for use with pastel, crayon, and charcoal.

Colored Pencil and Pastel

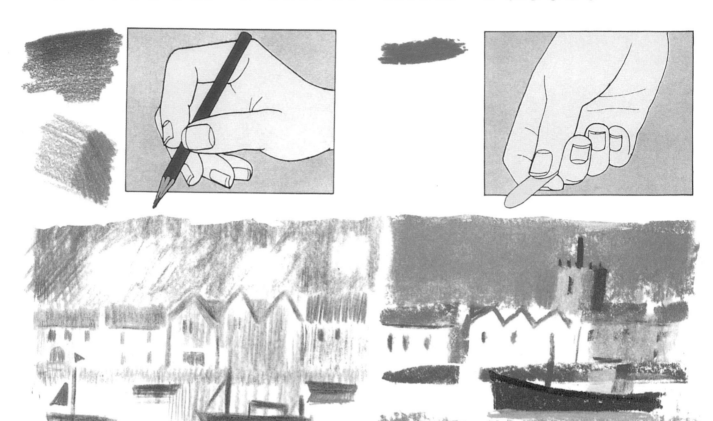

Colored pencils

Colored pencils are one of the most basic coloring tools. Many bright and wonderful colors are available. Artists like David Hockney use them. Although they are often used as colors in their own right, they mix and can be laid on top of one another to achieve different effects.

Chalk pastels

Chalk pastels are pure pigment bound together with gum. They blend well if you rub them with your finger—this is messy, but effective. Pastel can be put on smoothly with the side of the chalk, or quite thickly if you press firmly with the end. As with most materials, price and quality vary.

Colored pencil and wash

Water-soluble pencils are fun to experiment with. Lines drawn with them will blur to make an area of flat color if you lay a wash of clean water over them with a paint brush.

Color Theory

The six colors you can see in the color wheel on the right are divided into two groups. Red, yellow, and blue are called the primary colors. Orange, green, and purple are the secondary colors, and are a mix of the two primaries on either side.

Nearly all colors can be mixed from the primaries. The more colors that are mixed together, the duller the result. The colors opposite each other on the color wheel are known as complementaries. When placed side by side, they bring out the best in each other.

▲ "Make a color wheel for yourself with primary and secondary colors. Then try again, blending the secondaries from your primary colors."

Colors can be mixed in various ways. In crosshatching, shades of colored pencil are laid on top of each other.

Colors appear darker or lighter, depending on how hard you press down with your pencil or crayon.

Strokes of yellow wax crayon laid over blue produce a light green. Blue laid over yellow makes a darker green.

Wax crayons can be blended with a finger. If colors are rubbed too much, they will get dirty.

Felt marker colors can be blended by overlapping groups of tiny dots. This technique is used in color printing.

Basics: Line, Tone, and Texture

The project here is to try out line, tone, and texture separately. Then you can combine them in a single drawing. Find a subject you want to explore. You may wish to work from a photograph of your pet or your favorite animal, perhaps.

Taking a line for a walk

Lines are used to describe the shape of objects. By varying the thickness of your lines you can show all that is necessary to capture your subject. A lot can be left to the imagination.

Showing light and dark

The tone of an object is its darkness or lightness relative to other things. The cat in the middle picture below is darker than the rug, which is a lighter tone. But the tone of an object also changes depending on how light falls on it. By shading parts of your drawing, you can indicate these variations in tone, (see top right).

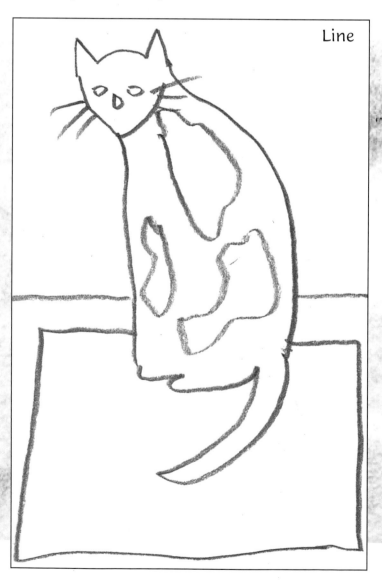

Line

Tone

Texture

"As you can see, the drawings for this project can be kept simple. In your final drawing (above), try to combine all three techniques in one image."

What is it made of?

If your drawings have texture, they will be rich, varied, and exciting to look at. The texture of your pencils or crayons on rough paper also helps to convey the actual texture (left) of your subject, like the hairiness of the cat.

White paper is part of your picture

In the line drawing, the lines enclose areas of white paper. In the tone drawing, the areas of white represent the lightest tone. In the texture drawing, the white areas form a contrast with the marks that cover the rest of the paper.

11

Basics: Finding the Form

An artist sometimes stalks his or her subject, slowly moving in on it. You can't always get things right the first time. Sometimes it is necessary to work in a very general way at first and gradually approach the finished result.

Feeling your way

For this project, choose a simple object, such as a tin can or a box. Look at it carefully. Take a pencil and sketch it

loosely (1). Go over and over your drawing with soft lines until the shape you want begins to appear (2). Be very free at this stage as mistakes can be erased later. Gradually feel your way toward the finished drawing.

Drawing with X-ray eyes

Try to think of your subject as transparent. Draw what you know is there in addition to what you can see. In the first drawing below, the whole bottom of the tin can is drawn in, although only part can be seen. At the second stage, the form of the tin can becomes clearer. Tones begin to be defined.

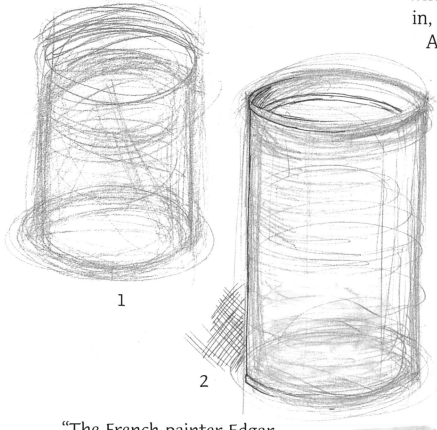

1

2

3

"The French painter Edgar Degas said that the artist does not draw what he sees, but what he must make others see. Try to bear this in mind when deciding which details to include in your drawing."

Basic three-dimensional forms

From the shapes pictured here, more complex shapes can be built. Most of what we see around us can be drawn from these simple beginnings. Make a collection of objects from around your home that are similar to, or based on, these forms. Practice drawing these shapes, which form the basis for many of the other projects in this book.

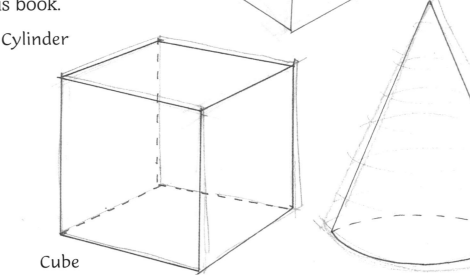

Pyramid

Sphere

Cone

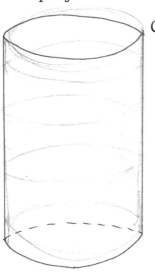

Cylinder

Cube

Drawing to a conclusion

Once you have the basic form right, start to notice how the light falls on it and where shadows appear. The last stage can be done with a soft pencil that produces a dark line, with dark crayon, conté, or pastel, or with pen and ink.

Try different kinds of shading techniques to convey the texture and tone of your subject. Crosshatching, dots, and lines running around the form can all help convey the shape and character of your subject, as shown in the final drawing (3).

Practicing forms

The more you practice drawing, the easier it becomes. Once you are familiar with this way of drawing, you can go on to do anything you like in the same way. Practice this method on other simple forms, like the ones that appear above. You can decide for yourself how much detail to put in.

Don't forget that sometimes you can overdraw. You will probably have to overwork a few drawings to find the right moment to stop. A fresh and lively drawing can be more interesting to look at than one that is overworked.

Basics: Light and Shade

Imagine drawing a bowl of fruit and making it so lifelike that people feel hungry just looking at it! It is possible, with a bit of practice, to give your drawings a real depth and solidity. One of the keys to this is the use of light and shadow. Everything has a light and a dark side, and usually an area that is in between the two.

Throwing light on the subject
Take the subject of your previous project, and a flashlight or lamp with a beam of light that you can direct. Light up your object and study the shadows. You'll notice one shadow on the side of the object itself, making it look solid, and one that is the shadow cast by the object onto the surface on which it is standing.

There is no light without shadow
Make a collection of objects based on the forms on the previous page. Shine a light on them and practice seeing and drawing the forms with their shadows. Move your source of light around and watch the shadows change. The effects are demonstrated below in black and gray felt-tip marker. The gray areas show the middle or half-tone.

Although an object generally gets darker as less light falls on it, there is often a lighter part just before the outer edge. This is because light has bounced back from another surface (the table on which the objects have been placed, for example). It lights the object from behind. This is reflected light.

Be a town planner

Most of what we see around us in the world is made up of simple shapes. Imagine you've been asked to design a town. Think of all the shapes of buildings you could design using the basic forms. What vehicles can you visualize driving through the streets?

Where is your sun?

Draw in the outlines of your forms first. Then decide where the sun is (it may not actually appear in your drawing, but the effects of it will).

▲ "In my felt-tip marker drawing, the sun appears quite low in the sky, and casts long shadows. Windows and other details can make your sketch more interesting."

The position of the sun determines where the shadows fall and how long they are. Shadows get longer as the sun goes down. Once you have finished, look at how real buildings in sunlight compare with those you have drawn. Yours might be better!

Basics: Perspective

Perspective is a way of drawing the three-dimensional world on a flat piece of paper. There are three techniques for showing perspective.

Linear perspective
In this technique, lines that in fact run parallel to one another appear to meet at a point on the horizon known as vanishing point.

Overlapping

Overlapping perspective
When one object is in front of another, the object in the foreground masks part of the one behind.

Linear

Tonal perspective
Strong, dark marks separate the foreground of a drawing from the softer lines of the background. So, differences in tone can make parts of a drawing seem closer or farther away.

All three techniques appear in the picture on the opposite page. Practice each technique separately before you put them all together.

Tonal

Test out this theory by looking around you and making drawings of your own.

▲ "My main drawing shows the three techniques in combination. The figures show the technique of overlapping. The street is shown to disappear into the background through the use of linear perspective. Tones and textures are more pronounced in the foreground, so this area appears closest to us."

Do we need rules?

These rules were established several hundred years ago to help show perspective. Today, some artists understand the rules and make use of them. Some understand the rules and choose not to use them; others get by without knowing about them at all. The rules are given here so that you can understand them and decide whether or not you want to use them. The best way of practicing perspective is to observe your surroundings carefully and put down on paper the things you notice.

Basics: Composition

Composition is about rearranging things and ordering them in a new way that seems more balanced and harmonious. Here, you can test this out for yourself.

The artist Paul Cézanne would spend hours setting up his still-life subjects, even using coins to tip up bowls and jars so he could see inside more easily.

By the time he had started work on a picture, he had practically finished! His subject already looked exactly as he wanted it to in the final work. How did he know what he wanted?

What feels right for you?
Creating your own picture by trial and error will give you a good feel for composition. Make a collection of household objects.

Which way up?
Your drawing paper has a particular shape. You can, of course, decide which way up to hold it, making a picture that is wide or tall. Before you begin, spend some time imagining how the composition will look on paper. A composition is a group of shapes arranged in certain positions. Try some unusual ones, even those you think may look strange. Experiment with a series of arrangements on a table or even the floor. Try out compositions that you think will look unbalanced: top-heavy, cramped, or too spaced out, as well as ones that look balanced. Unconventional compositions can produce good results.

Choose those you feel might go well together in a picture. In the examples above there are five, but you might like to start with more. You could then discard some as you go along.

▲ "Compositions can look orderly, comfortable, or plain crazy! My three examples here are quite sensible, but you don't have to be!"

Trying out composition

Rearrange your objects and draw a series of pictures based on them. Test out the idea that a pleasing or harmonious composition is a balanced one. In a balanced composition, a single large object can appear to equal two smaller ones. Perhaps you could draw one or more of the objects so that they only appear partially in your picture. Many artists have used this technique deliberately, to make unexpected compositions.

Drawing the Head

Over the next pages we will examine how to draw faces step by step, looking at the proportions of the head, the features, and finally, how to achieve a likeness.

The shape of the head

Viewed from the front, the head is an egg-shaped form sitting on the neck. Practice drawing the shape of the head and positioning the features within it, as described in the box below. Use the method described on pages 12-13 to feel your way toward the form and proportions of the head.

A study from life

Once you can manage these proportions, ask a friend to sit for you. Perhaps you can draw each other at the same time. Draw your subject's head from side, front, and three-quarter views. Don't worry about getting a perfect likeness just yet.

▶ "My simple line drawing could be taken further by adding shading, but I felt it might become confused. Sometimes it's best to quit while you are ahead, rather than risk going on for too long."

Making the headlines

The first thing to notice is that the eyes come halfway down the head, and not higher up. The end of the nose lies midway between eyes and chin; the mouth comes halfway between nose and chin. There is the width of an eye between the eyes, and also across the bottom of the nose. On the sides of the head, the ears should be placed midway between the eyes and the nose.

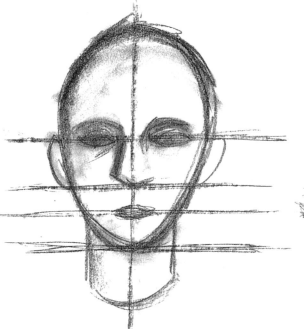

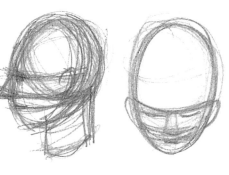

Features and Expressions

We all have two eyes, two ears, a nose, and a mouth. These features conform to certain shapes: the nose is a triangular form, eyes are oval in shape. But no two people's features are the same.

On the opposite page, the features are drawn step by step. The first drawing in each sequence shows the basic form. The second shows the character developing. In the third, shading has been added to emphasize the form.

A subject for your portrait

Once you are familiar with drawing features and expressions, it's time to try to achieve a likeness. This is fun as long as no one minds whether or not you succeed. When Oliver Cromwell had his portrait painted, he insisted that he was shown, "warts and all." The artist was lucky on this occasion, as people can be sensitive about how they look!

Getting a likeness

A likeness depends on drawing the features and capturing how they go together. The rest of the face is almost as important as the features. The distance between the eyes, or the gap between nose and mouth, vary as much as the shape of the nose. It's important to get these details right.

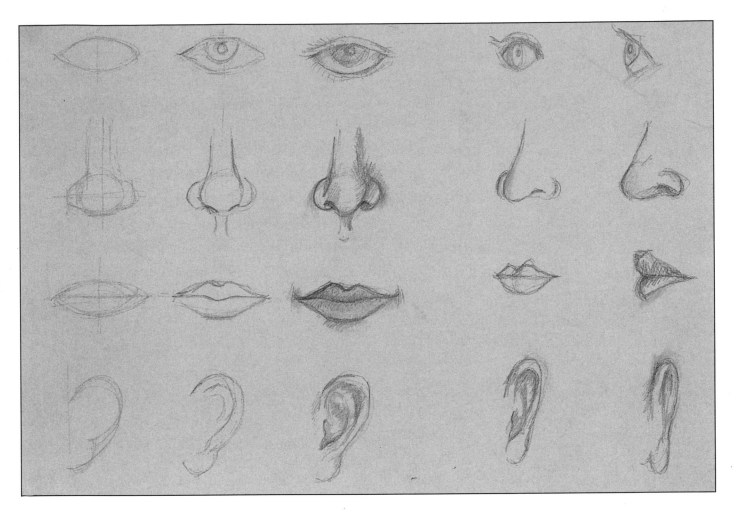

▲ "Above, I have sketched front, three-quarter, and side views of the same features. Crosshatching adds solidity."

Putting on expressions

The drawings on the left show the subject of the previous page in different moods: first sad, then happy, and slightly puzzled. The features, and even the hair, droop downward in the sad face, as though there is no energy to support them. Enthusiasm lifts the lines upward in the happy face. In a puzzled face, the lines are undecided and waver in different directions. See how your face changes as you practice looking delighted, annoyed, or tired.

The Human Figure

Getting things in proportion

Proportion is about comparing the size of one thing to another. Body length is often measured in relation to the head. The average adult is seven heads tall. The torso is three heads, and divides into thirds at the nipple line and navel. The top of the legs to the soles of the feet also measures three heads. Children's heads are larger in proportion to the rest of their bodies. With your arms stretched out sideways, the distance between your fingertips is the same as your height—try it!

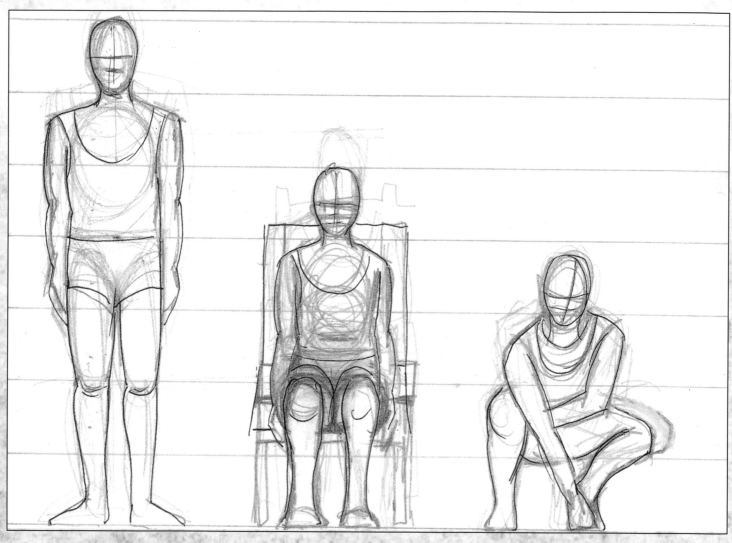

▲ "Above, I have drawn the proportions of the standing figure. You might want to copy this first. Try it again from memory. Then, check the measurements against a real person."

▲ "The seated figure shows how two heads have been 'lost' from the height; the space from hips to knees has become foreshortened. Again, check this against the real thing."

▲ "The crouching figure is more complicated, because the top half is also foreshortened as it leans toward you. The legs are foreshortened differently. Can you see how?"

Foreshortening

Parts of the body appear larger or smaller, depending on whether they are near or far from the person looking at them. If someone's leg or arm is pointing directly at you, part of its length will be hidden. This is known as *foreshortening*. You can see it in the drawings on the left.

Practicing foreshortening

Foreshortening is far more dramatic when you look at a figure from an unusual angle. As shown in the drawings above and bottom left, a person with his arm outstretched toward you, or lying down, will seem to have a huge hand or big feet. It takes alot of practice to get these things right. The middle drawing is of the artist looking down at his own body. Why not try a drawing like this?

People on the Move

"Don't try to run before you can walk," the saying goes, and it's true that if you overreach yourself in the real world, you hurt yourself. However, with drawing, there's no harm in taking risks.

A sense of balance

You can learn a lot about how the figure moves by trying it yourself! As you walk or run, try to be aware of what happens to your body. Feel how your weight shifts from one leg to the other, so that each leg in turn holds the body up as the other swings forward to take the next step.

Let's get moving

The illustrations below show a figure running. Each part of the sequence flows into the next. Notice how at each stage, the running figure is balanced by the different positions of the limbs.

The project takes this idea farther. Find a photograph of someone running, in a newspaper or magazine. Photographs can be confusing, so choose one where you can really see what's happening. Make a drawing based on the photo you've chosen.

Before and after

Before photography was invented, artists had to rely on their eyes and their imagination. The next step is to try and imagine the positions the runner would be in before and after the photograph was taken. Make sketches of these positions on either side of your first drawing.

Having finished the project, try drawing people moving around you. Get used to working quickly and you will be surprised how your drawing can improve.

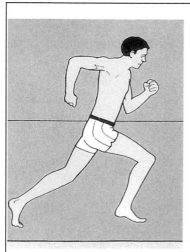
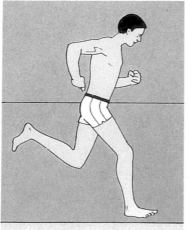
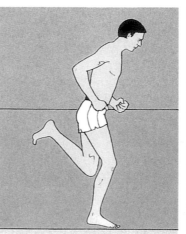
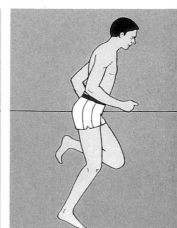

▲ "Here is an example of this project with my attempts at guessing "before and after" positions for my runner. I've tried to get a feeling of energy and movement into the drawings so that, unlike the photograph I drew from, my sketches aren't frozen and still. Try it yourself and see how you do!"

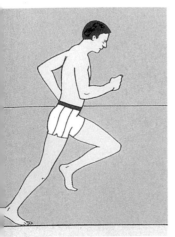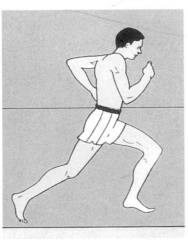

A man on the run

The illustrations of the running man are included for information, rather than as examples of how you should draw. They offer an explanation of what happens when we run. Your drawings should convey information and a sense of movement. Try making your pencil move across the paper enthusiastically, to show the runner's energy.

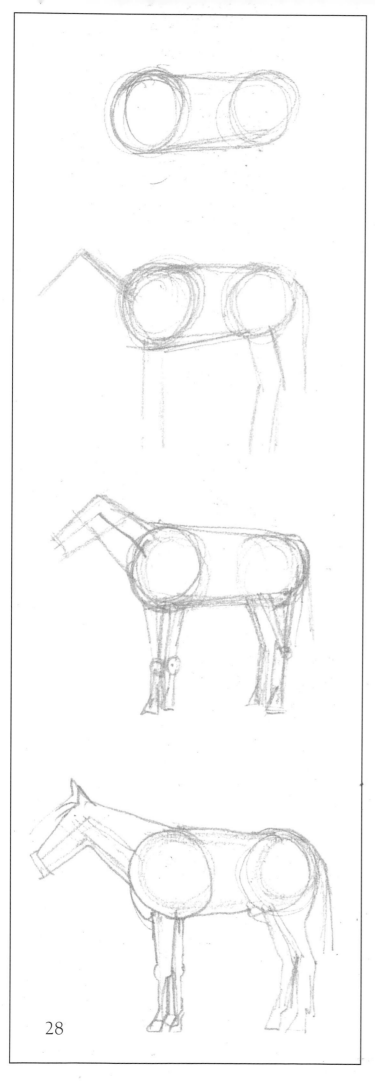

Animal Studies

The variety in the natural world provides a constant source of inspiration to the artist. Drawing animals provides a great chance to experiment with lines and mark-making. The texture of an animal's coat is very important. Let your eyes enjoy the softness of cats, the sleekness of horses, and the prickliness of porcupines.

◄ "In this example you can see how a drawing can "evolve," or emerge gradually. The basic shapes develop step by step into a particular horse. At each stage, more detail is added until, finally, the animal has its own special presence. Follow this sequence of drawings to produce your own version of a horse. You might want to put the figure of a rider on the horse's back to make your drawing more interesting."

▼ "In the final stages, I added tone to make my horse look more solid and to complete my picture."

Caught on the hop

Below, you can see an example of how an animal moves. Look at the animal and allow your pencil to follow the forms in front of you without looking at the paper. Make a sequence of drawings as the animal moves. When it changes position, if it is only a slight change, keep the same drawing going.

If it changes into a different pose entirely, begin another drawing. Return to the previous one when the original pose is taken up again.

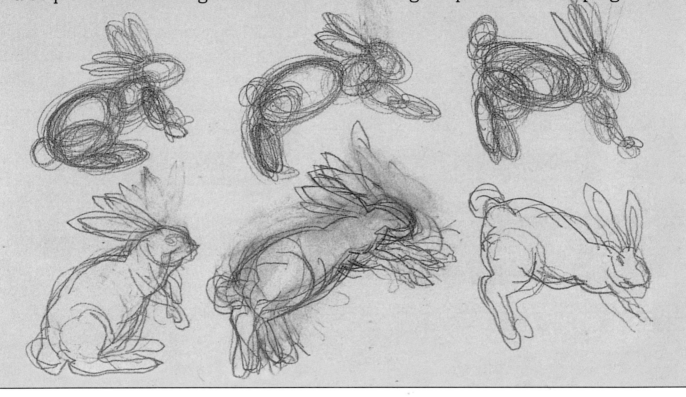

Back to basics

The simple shapes we studied earlier are the basis for animal forms, and can be used to make your drawings convincing. The drawings on the left show how the figure of a horse evolves from a few basic shapes. Try this with your own drawing and then try it with other animals. What basic shapes might develop into a cow, a dog, or a cat?

Animals don't stay still

The problem with drawing living creatures is that they rarely stand still and pose for you. As with drawimg a moving human figure, the combination of photographs, your imagination, and your observations can work very well.

Field studies

Don't be afraid to draw from real life whenever possible. Even if your drawing doesn't have a textbook likeness, it may well have a special quality. Use a rough sketchbook, the less expensive the better, so you will not feel that what you do has to be perfect. Learn to draw quickly and directly, and your drawings will take on a life of their own.

Presentation

Finished drawings, particularly those in charcoal, conté, or pastel, should be sprayed with fixative to protect them. Use fixative in a well ventilated room. Be careful not to get any in your eyes. Try to spray your drawings evenly.

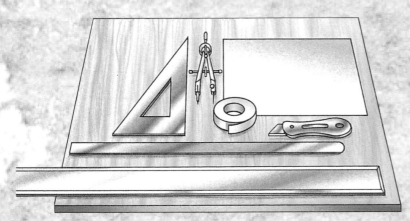

For the record
Put the date on your drawings, and possibly also the place where they were drawn. One day you'll look back and notice how your work has changed over the years.

Mounting your work
Mounting your drawings can make them look better than you ever thought possible. In general, steer away from brightly colored mounts; white and cream mounts are usually effective. Measure the area for your mount accurately with a ruler, and cut it out carefully with a knife.

Drawing with a mount
Mounts can be useful while drawing if you are using brush and ink, or if you are working very freely with any material. Before you begin, place a mount on your paper, framing the area in which you intend to draw. Allow your drawing to go over the edges of the mount. Once you have finished, remove the mount. You'll find a clean edge framing your work which will make it look neat.

Practical Tips

Keeping equipment safe

Keep your paper, pencils, and drawing pads together in one place. Keep your paper in a drawer where it can lie flat and will not get creased or soiled.

Drawing large and free

Try drawing on a large scale. Don't feel that your work has to be small and detailed. You may find that you are able to express yourself more completely if you can move your arm freely. If you are the sort of person who enjoys working on large drawings, you may find it easier to draw standing up at an easel.

More about paper

There are many types of paper. Watercolor paper is good to work on, particularly in pastel, conté, crayon, or charcoal. Its rough surface will make your strokes look broken and bold. Charcoal paper has a delicate ribbed surface. It allows you to blend your strokes and create velvety tones.

Drawing with an eraser

An eraser can be used as a drawing tool. Try shading in an area of your paper with pencil or charcoal. Then draw with your eraser. You have effectively drawn in the areas you would usually leave out.

Drawing outside

To draw outside, find a comfortable spot to sit, from where your subject is visible. If it is windy you'll need to tape your paper down. Hold your sketch pad so that your page is in the shade.

Getting ideas

Keep a scrapbook of clippings as ideas for future work. Visit art galleries to learn from other artists. You can learn about different techniques from etchings in museums. Carry a sketchbook with you for noting down ideas, and making quick sketches for later use.

Index